Ruby Programming Nice Guide for Beginners

Setting Up Your Ruby Programming Environment

By

Aulay Braidy

Copyright@2023

Table of Contents

CHAPTER 1

Introduction

1.1 What is Ruby

Ruby is a dynamic, high-level, and versatile programming language that was created by Yukihiro Matsumoto in the mid-1990s. It is known for its simplicity and productivity, making it an excellent choice for both beginners and experienced programmers. Ruby is often referred to as a "scripting language" because of its ease of use and its ability to execute code quickly and efficiently.

One of the defining features of Ruby is its emphasis on readability and elegant syntax. Matsumoto designed Ruby with the principle of making the language natural and easy to understand, which has led to a community of developers who prioritize writing code that is not only functional but also beautiful.

Ruby is an interpreted language, which means that you don't need to compile your code before running it. This makes the development process faster and more flexible, allowing you to experiment and iterate quickly.

Ruby is also known for its object-oriented programming (OOP) capabilities. In Ruby, everything is an object, and you can create and manipulate objects easily. This makes it a great language for building complex, modular, and reusable code.

Ruby's ecosystem is supported by a vast library of open-source packages and gems that extend its functionality.

This rich ecosystem simplifies many common programming tasks, from working with databases to creating web applications.

1.2 Why Learn Ruby

There are several compelling reasons to learn Ruby:

1. **Beginner-Friendly**: Ruby's elegant and human-readable syntax makes it an excellent choice for beginners. If you're just starting your programming journey, Ruby can be a gentle introduction to coding concepts.

2. **Versatile**: Ruby is a versatile language that can be used for a wide range of applications. It's commonly used for web

development, automation, data analysis, and more.

3. **Strong Community**: Ruby has a vibrant and supportive community of developers.

4. **Career Opportunities**: Ruby is still widely used in the industry, particularly in web development with the Ruby on Rails framework. Learning Ruby can open up job opportunities as a web developer, software engineer, or full-stack developer.

5. **Coding Principles**: Ruby teaches important programming principles, such as object-oriented programming (OOP) and good coding practices. These principles are

transferable to other programming languages.

6. **Creativity and Productivity**: Ruby's focus on developer happiness and productivity encourages creative problem-solving.

1.3 Setting Up Your Ruby Environment

Before you start coding in Ruby, you'll need to set up your development environment. This typically involves the following steps:

1. **Install Ruby**: Depending on your operating system, you may need to install Ruby. There are various ways to do this, including using package managers like **apt**, **brew**, or

downloading it directly from the official website.

2. **Text Editor or IDE**: Choose a text editor or integrated development environment (IDE) for writing your Ruby code. Some popular options include Visual Studio Code, Sublime Text, and RubyMine.

3. **Version Control**: Consider using version control software like Git to manage your code and collaborate with others.

4. **Package Manager**: Ruby uses a package manager called RubyGems to manage libraries and dependencies. Familiarize yourself with how to use it to install gems.

5. **Documentation**: Explore Ruby's official documentation

and other learning resources. Online tutorials, books, and forums can be valuable for your learning journey.

6. **Practice**: Start writing simple Ruby programs to practice what you've learned. Experiment with different aspects of the language to gain hands-on experience.

CHAPTER 2

Getting Started with Ruby

2.1 Your First Ruby Program

Getting started with Ruby involves creating and running your first Ruby program, which is often referred to as a "Hello World" program. This simple program is used to ensure that your Ruby environment is set up correctly and that you can run Ruby code.

- **Print Output**: Ruby uses the **puts** or **print** statements to display output to the console.

- **Comments**: Comments are used to add explanations and

notes to your code. They are not executed and are purely for human readability.

- **Running Your Code**: exploring how to execute your Ruby program from the command line or an integrated development environment (IDE). Running your program allows you to see the output and check for any errors.

2.2 Variables and Data Types:

- **Variables**: Variables are used to store and manage data in a program. we will learn about variable naming conventions, how to declare and assign values to variables, and the scope of variables (local, instance, class, and global).

- **Data Types**: Ruby has several fundamental data types, including integers, floats (decimal numbers), strings (text), booleans (true or false), arrays (ordered lists), and hashes (key-value pairs).

- **Type Conversion**: Sometimes, you may need to convert data from one type to another.

- **Immutable and Mutable**: Some data types in Ruby are immutable, meaning their values cannot be changed after creation, while others are mutable, allowing you to modify their contents.

These fundamental concepts of variables and data types is crucial for writing effective Ruby code. They provide the building blocks for storing and manipulating data in your programs, which is essential for any programming language.

2.3 Basic Input and Output

- **Output**: Ruby provides various methods for displaying information to the user. We will explore how to use these methods to show results, messages, or data on the screen. Output is essential for communicating with users or other parts of a program.

- **Input**: Interacting with the user or receiving external data is a fundamental aspect of programming. Ruby allows you to gather input from users or external sources. This input can then be processed and used within your program.

- **Standard Streams**: Ruby uses standard input (**STDIN**) and standard output (**STDOUT**) as channels for communication.

- **Formatting**: While not delving into the specifics, basic formatting techniques are used to present information in a human-readable way. Proper formatting enhances the user's experience when interacting with your programs.

2.4 Comments in Ruby

Comments are crucial for code documentation and improving code readability. We will explore the following aspects of comments in Ruby:

- **Purpose**: Comments serve as explanatory notes within your code. They are not executed and do not affect the program's functionality. Instead, they provide information to developers (including your future self) about the purpose of code segments, explanations of complex logic, or reminders.

- **Single-Line Comments**: Ruby allows single-line comments, which start with a designated character and continue until the end of the line.

- **Multi-Line Comments**: While Ruby does not have dedicated multi-line comment syntax, there are conventions for achieving multi-line comments using multiple single-line comments. These are often employed for longer explanations or to temporarily disable code blocks.

- **Comment Best Practices**: Importance of writing clear and concise comments, adhering to established comment conventions, and ensuring that comments remain up to date as your code evolves.

Effective commenting is a vital skill for developers, as it helps others (and yourself) understand your code's purpose and functionality. It also aids

in debugging and maintaining code in
the long run.

CHAPTER 3
Control Flow

3.1 Conditional Statements (if, else, elsif)

Conditional statements allow your Ruby program to make decisions and take different actions based on specific conditions.

- **if Statements**: **if** statement, allows you to execute a block of code if a specified condition is true.

- **else Statements**: When you want to provide an alternative action to take when the initial condition is false, you can use the **else** statement.

- **elsif Statements**: In cases where you need to evaluate multiple conditions sequentially, you can use **elsif** statements. These are used to check additional conditions if the initial **if** condition is false.

- **Nested Conditionals**: you can nest conditional statements within one another to handle complex decision-making situations.

3.2 Loops (while, for, until)

Loops are used to execute a block of code repeatedly, either while a condition is true or for a specific number of times.

- **while Loops**: The **while** loop executes a block of code as long as a specified condition remains true.

- **for Loops**: The **for** loop is used to iterate over a collection (e.g., an array or a range) and execute a block of code for each item in the collection.

- **until Loops**: The **until** loop is similar to the **while** loop but executes the block of code until a specified condition becomes true.

- **Loop Control Keywords**: Ruby provides control keywords like **break** and **next** that allow you to exit a loop prematurely or skip specific iterations. These keywords can enhance the functionality of loops.

3.3 Case Statements

The **case** statement, also known as a switch statement in other programming languages, is used to evaluate a value against multiple possible conditions and execute code blocks accordingly.

- **Case Expression**: **case** statement are used to compare a value (or expression) against a series of when conditions.

- **When Clauses**: Each **when** clause represents a possible condition to check against the case expression. When a match is found, the corresponding code block is executed.

- **Default Case**: You can include a **else** or **when else** clause to specify what should happen if none of the when conditions match the case expression.

Control flow and how to use conditional statements, loops, and case statements is essential for creating programs that can make decisions and execute specific actions based on varying conditions and input data.

CHAPTER 4

Ruby Data Structures

4.1 Arrays

Arrays in Ruby are ordered collections of objects. Key characteristics of arrays include:

- **Ordered**: Arrays maintain the order in which elements are added. You can access elements by their position or index within the array.

- **Mutable**: You can add, remove, or modify elements in an array after it's created.

- **Heterogeneous**: An array can hold objects of different data types, including integers, strings, and even other arrays.

- **Zero-Based Indexing**: Ruby uses zero-based indexing, which means the first element of an array is at index 0, the second at index 1, and so on.

- **Common Array Operations**: Arrays support various operations, such as appending elements, removing elements, finding the length, and iterating through elements.

4.2 Hashes

Hashes, also known as associative arrays or dictionaries in other languages, are key-value data structures in Ruby. Key points about hashes include:

- **Key-Value Pairs**: A hash consists of key-value pairs, where each key is associated with a specific value. Keys are typically unique within a hash.

- **Unordered**: Unlike arrays, hashes are not ordered collections. The order of key-value pairs may not be preserved.

- **Fast Lookups**: Hashes provide fast lookup times based on the key. You can quickly retrieve the associated value for a given key.

- **Symbol Keys**: Symbols are commonly used as keys in hashes due to their immutability and efficiency.

- **Common Hash Operations**: You can add new key-value

pairs, update existing values,
delete entries, and iterate
through the keys and values in
a hash.

4.3 Strings

Strings are sequences of characters
and are fundamental for working with
text in Ruby. Key aspects of strings
include:

- **Immutable**: Strings in Ruby
  are immutable, meaning you
  cannot change the characters in
  an existing string. Instead,
  operations on strings typically
  create new strings.

- **Double-Quoted vs. Single-
  Quoted**: Ruby allows you to
  create strings using either
  double quotes (") or single

quotes ('). Double-quoted strings support string interpolation (embedding variable values) and escape sequences.

- **Encoding**: Ruby supports various character encodings, allowing you to work with different character sets and languages.

- **String Methods**: Ruby provides a rich set of methods for manipulating strings, including functions for concatenation, splitting, searching, and replacing substrings.

- **Regular Expressions**: Ruby has robust support for regular expressions, which are powerful tools for pattern matching and text manipulation within strings.

These data structures—arrays, hashes, and strings—is crucial for many programming tasks. Arrays are used for ordered collections of items, hashes for key-value pairs, and strings for text processing. Being familiar with their properties and common operations will enable you to work with data effectively in Ruby.

CHAPTER 5

Methods and Functions

5.1 Defining and Calling Methods

- **Method Definition**: In Ruby, methods are blocks of code that perform a specific task. You define methods using the **def** keyword, followed by the method name, parameters (if any), and the method body enclosed in **do...end** or curly braces {}.

- **Method Invocation**: To execute a method, you call it by its name followed by parentheses (). If the method doesn't take any arguments, you can omit the parentheses.

- **Reusability**: Methods allow you to write reusable pieces of code. Instead of duplicating the same code multiple times, you can define a method and call it whenever needed.

5.2 Function Parameters and Return Values

- **Parameters**: Methods can accept input data through parameters. Parameters are variables that act as placeholders for values provided when the method is called. You define parameters

within the parentheses
following the method name.

- **Arguments**: When you call a
method, you provide actual
values, known as arguments,
that are assigned to the
corresponding parameters.

- **Return Values**: Methods can
return a value to the caller. The
return keyword is used to
specify what value the method
should return. If no **return**
statement is used, the method
returns the value of the last
expression evaluated.

- **Implicit Return**: Ruby often
uses implicit return, meaning
the last expression's result is
automatically returned without
a **return** statement. This

simplifies code and enhances readability.

5.3 Scope and Variables

- **Local Variables**: Variables declared within a method have local scope, meaning they are only accessible within that method. Local variables have limited visibility and are not accessible from outside the method.

- **Global Variables**: Global variables have a global scope, making them accessible throughout the entire program. However, it's considered best practice to minimize the use of global variables to avoid unintended side effects.

- **Instance Variables**: Instance variables begin with the **@** symbol and are used within classes to store state that can be shared among multiple methods within an object instance. They have instance-level scope.

- **Class Variables**: Class variables begin with **@@** and are shared among all instances of a class. They have class-level scope.

- **Constants**: Constants in Ruby are declared in all uppercase letters and have class-level scope. They are typically used for values that should not change throughout the program.

- **Scope and Shadowing**: Understanding scope is crucial to avoid variable shadowing,

where a local variable in an
inner scope has the same name
as a variable in an outer scope,
potentially leading to
unexpected behavior.

CHAPTER 6

Object-Oriented Programming in Ruby

6.1 Classes and Objects

- **Classes**: In Ruby, a class is a blueprint or template for creating objects. It defines the structure and behavior that its objects will have. A class encapsulates data (attributes) and behaviors (methods) related to a particular concept or entity.

- **Objects**: Objects are instances of classes. They are created from a class definition and represent individual instances of that class. Each object has its own set of attributes and can perform actions defined by the class's methods.

- **Attributes**: In OOP, attributes (also called properties or instance variables) store data specific to each object. They define the object's state. Attributes are typically declared within the class and can have different values for different objects.

- **Methods**: Methods in a class define the behavior or actions that objects of that class can perform. Methods can read and modify the object's attributes and can interact with other objects and classes.

- **Encapsulation**: One of the key principles of OOP is encapsulation, which means bundling data (attributes) and methods that operate on that data into a single unit (a class). Encapsulation helps control access to an object's internal state and ensures data integrity.

6.2 Constructors and Instance Variables

- **Constructors**: In Ruby, the constructor method is called **initialize**. It is automatically called when a new object is created from a class. The **initialize** method is used to set initial values for the object's attributes. It can take parameters to initialize attributes based on provided values.

- **Instance Variables**: Instance variables are used to store data that belongs to an object. They are prefixed with @ and are accessible throughout the object's methods. Instance variables have object-level scope, meaning each object has its own set of instance variables.

- **Getter and Setter Methods**: To access and modify instance variables, getter and setter methods are often used. Getter methods provide read-only access to instance variables, while setter methods allow you to modify them. In Ruby, you can define custom getter and setter methods, or use

shorthand methods like
attr_reader, **attr_writer**, and
attr_accessor.

- **Instance Methods**: Instance methods are defined within a class and operate on the instance variables and other data associated with an object of that class. These methods can read and modify the object's state and perform various actions.

6.3 Methods in Classes

- **Instance Methods**: Methods defined within a class are typically instance methods. These methods operate on individual objects (instances) of the class. They can access and manipulate instance variables

and perform actions specific to
each object.

- **Class Methods**: While most
methods in a class are instance
methods, Ruby also supports
class methods. Class methods
are called on the class itself,
rather than on instances of the
class. They are defined using
the **self**-keyword or the class
name and are often used for
tasks that are not specific to
individual objects.

- **Private and Public Methods**:
Ruby provides access control
modifiers like **private** and
public to manage method
visibility. Methods marked as
private can only be called from
within the class, while **public**
methods can be called from
outside the class. This helps

encapsulate and protect the internal workings of a class.

6.4 Inheritance and Polymorphism

- **Inheritance**: Inheritance is a key concept in OOP that allows you to create new classes based on existing classes. The new class (subclass or derived class) inherits attributes and methods from the existing class (superclass or base class). Inheritance promotes code reuse and hierarchy.

- **Superclass and Subclass**: The superclass is the class from which another class inherits. The subclass is the class that inherits from the superclass.

Subclasses can add new attributes and methods, override existing methods, and specialize the behavior of the superclass.

- **Polymorphism**: Polymorphism is the ability of different objects to respond to the same method in their own unique way. It allows objects of different classes to be treated as instances of a common superclass, enabling flexibility and extensibility in your code.

- **Method Overriding**: Subclasses can override (redefine) methods inherited from the superclass to provide their own implementation. When a method is called on an object of the subclass, the overridden method in the subclass is executed instead of the superclass method.

- **Polymorphic Methods**: Polymorphism is often achieved through interfaces or abstract classes that define a common set of methods that subclasses must implement. This allows different classes to be used interchangeably in a polymorphic manner.

- **Duck Typing**: Ruby employs duck typing, which means that the type or class of an object is determined by its behavior (methods it responds to) rather than by its explicit type. This allows for flexible and dynamic programming.

CHAPTER 7

Exception Handling

7.1 Handling Errors with begin and rescue

- **Error Handling**: Exception handling is a mechanism in Ruby (and many other programming languages) that allows you to gracefully handle errors or exceptional situations that might occur during program execution.

- **begin and rescue**: In Ruby, you use a **begin** block to enclose the code that might raise an exception. The **rescue** block follows the **begin** block and specifies the code to execute when an exception is raised. You can have multiple **rescue** blocks to handle different types of exceptions.

- **Types of Exceptions**: Ruby provides a variety of built-in exception classes that represent different types of errors, such as **StandardError**, **TypeError**, **ZeroDivisionError**, etc. You can specify the type of exception you want to rescue in a **rescue** block.

- **ensure Block**: You can use an **ensure** block to specify code that should always be executed, whether or not an exception is raised. This is useful for tasks like resource cleanup.

- **Nested Exception Handling**: You can nest exception-handling constructs to handle exceptions at different levels of your code.

7.2 Raising Custom Exceptions

- **Custom Exceptions**: In addition to handling built-in exceptions, you can create your own custom exception classes by subclassing **StandardError** or one of its descendants. This allows you to define and raise exceptions that are specific to your application's needs.

- **raise Keyword**: You can use the **raise** keyword to explicitly raise an exception at a particular point in your code. This is useful when you want to signal an error condition or handle exceptional cases.

- **Exception Messages**: When raising custom exceptions, you can provide a descriptive message that explains the reason for the exception. This message can be helpful for debugging and error reporting.

- **Exception Hierarchy**: Custom exceptions can be organized into a hierarchy, just like the built-in exceptions in Ruby. You can create a base exception class and derive specific exceptions from it to represent different error scenarios in your application.

Exception handling is essential for robust and fault-tolerant programs. It allows you to gracefully handle errors, prevent unexpected program termination, and provide meaningful error messages to users or developers. Custom exceptions can help you tailor error handling to the specific needs of your application.

CHAPTER 8

Working with Files

8.1 Reading and Writing Files

- **File Operations**: In Ruby, you can perform various file operations, including reading from and writing to files. This is essential for tasks such as processing data files, generating reports, and managing configuration files.

- **Reading Files**: To read data from a file, you can use methods like **File.open** or **File.read**. Ruby provides different modes for reading files, such as read-only (**'r'**), read-write (**'r+'**), and more.

- **Writing Files**: To write data to a file, you can use methods like **File.open** with the write mode (**'w'**) or append mode (**'a'**). You can also specify binary mode (**'b'**) for working with non-text files.

- **Closing Files**: It's important to close files after you're done with them to free up system resources and ensure data integrity. You can use the **close** method or a block with **File.open** to automatically close files when you're finished.

- **Error Handling**: When working with files, it's important to handle potential errors, such as file not found, permission issues, or disk space problems. Proper error handling ensures your program responds gracefully to unexpected situations.

8.2 File Handling Best Practices

- **File Paths**: When specifying file paths, use platform-independent methods like **File.join** or the **Pathname** class to construct paths. This helps ensure your code works on different operating systems.

- **File Encoding**: Be aware of character encoding when working with text files. Specify the correct encoding when opening files to prevent encoding-related issues.

- **File Existence**: Before performing file operations, check whether the file exists using methods like **File.exist?**. This helps avoid errors when trying to access non-existent files.

- **Error Handling**: Implement robust error handling by using **begin** and **rescue** blocks to handle exceptions that may occur during file operations. This makes your code more resilient.

- **File Modes**: Choose the appropriate file mode (**'r'**, **'w'**, **'a'**, etc.) based on your intended file operation. Be cautious when using write modes, as they can overwrite existing data.

- **Buffers and Efficiency**: Consider using buffered I/O for improved efficiency when working with large files. Buffered I/O reduces the number of system calls and can improve performance.

- **Resource Management**: Use the **File** class methods like **File.open** with a block to ensure proper resource management. This way, the file is automatically closed when you're done.

- **Backup and Version Control**: When writing to files, consider implementing backup or version control mechanisms to preserve previous versions of the file in case of accidental data loss or corruption.

- **Security**: Be mindful of file permissions and security. Ensure that your code does not inadvertently expose sensitive data or allow unauthorized access to files.

- **Testing**: Write unit tests to verify that your file-handling code works as expected. Mock file operations in tests to ensure predictable behavior.

Working with files is a common task in many applications. Following best practices for file handling ensures that your code is robust, efficient, and reliable when dealing with input and output operations on files.

CHAPTER 9

Ruby Gems

9.1 Installing Gems

- **What Are Gems?**: Gems are packages or libraries in the Ruby programming language that provide pre-written code for various functionalities. Gems are used to extend Ruby's capabilities and simplify complex tasks.

- **Gem Management**: RubyGems is Ruby's package manager, and it allows you to easily install, update, and manage gems. To install a gem, you typically use the **gem install** command followed by

the gem's name. RubyGems
will automatically download
and install the gem along with
its dependencies.

- **Version Control**: You can
  specify the version of a gem
  you want to install by
  appending the version number
  to the gem's name. This helps
  ensure that your code works
  consistently, even if newer
  versions of the gem are
  released.

- **Gemfile and Bundler**: In many
  Ruby projects, you'll find a
  Gemfile that lists the required
  gems and their versions.
  Bundler is a tool used to
  manage gem dependencies
  based on the Gemfile. Running
  bundle install will install all

the required gems specified in
the Gemfile.

9.2 Using Popular Gems

- **Gem Documentation**: When
  using gems, it's important to refer
  to the gem's documentation to
  understand how to use it
  effectively. Gems typically have
  well-documented features,
  methods, and usage examples.

- **Popular Gems**: Ruby has a rich
  ecosystem of gems for various
  purposes, such as web
  development, database interaction,
  testing, and more. Some popular
  gems include:

  - **Ruby on Rails**: A web
    application framework that
    simplifies web development.

- **Devise**: A flexible and customizable authentication solution for Rails applications.

- **RSpec**: A popular testing framework for writing behavior-driven tests.

- **ActiveRecord**: The ORM (Object-Relational Mapping) library used in Rails for database interactions.

- **CarrierWave**: A gem for managing file uploads and attachments.

- **Sidekiq**: A background processing framework for running asynchronous tasks.

- **Community and Support**: When choosing and using gems, it's important to consider factors such as the gem's popularity, the activity of its community, and its maintenance status. Active and well-maintained gems are more likely to receive updates and bug fixes.

- **Version Compatibility**: Be mindful of gem version compatibility with your Ruby version and other gems in your project. Gem dependencies can sometimes conflict, so it's important to ensure they work well together.

- **Security**: Keep your gems up to date to benefit from security patches and bug fixes. Regularly check for gem updates and consider using tools like Bundler Audit to identify and fix security vulnerabilities.

Using gems in your Ruby projects can save you a significant amount of time and effort by leveraging pre-built functionality and libraries created by the Ruby community. When selecting and using gems, always consider the specific requirements of your project and follow best practices for gem management and security.

CHAPTER 10

Ruby on Rails

10.1 What is Ruby on Rails

- **Ruby on Rails**: Ruby on Rails, commonly known as Rails, is a powerful and popular open-source web application framework written in the Ruby programming language. It was created by David Heinemeier Hansson and was first released in 2005. Rails is designed to make web development faster, easier, and more productive by providing a structured and opinionated framework.

- **Convention over Configuration (CoC)**: One of the key principles of Rails is Convention over Configuration. Rails follows a set of conventions and best practices, which means developers don't have to spend time configuring every aspect of their application. This allows for rapid development and consistent code structure.

- **Don't Repeat Yourself (DRY)**: Rails promotes the DRY principle, encouraging developers to write reusable code and avoid duplicating logic. This leads to cleaner and more maintainable code.

- **Model-View-Controller (MVC) Architecture**: Rails follows the MVC architectural pattern, separating an application into three main components: Models (representing data and business logic), Views (handling user interface and presentation), and Controllers (managing user requests and handling communication between Models and Views).

- **Gem Ecosystem**: Rails has a rich ecosystem of gems (packages or libraries) that extend its functionality. These gems cover a wide range of tasks, from authentication and authorization to database management and more. Rails developers can leverage these gems to build robust web applications more efficiently.

10.2 Setting Up a Ruby on Rails Project

- **Installation**: To set up a Ruby on Rails project, you first need to ensure that you have Ruby and the Rails gem installed on your system. You can use the **gem install rails** command to install Rails globally.

- **Creating a New Project**: Rails provides a command-line tool called **rails** to generate a new project. You can create a new project by running **rails new project_name**, where **project_name** is the name of your application.

- **Directory Structure**: A Rails project has a well-defined directory structure that follows conventions. Key directories include **app** (for application code), **config** (for configuration files), **db** (for database-related files), and **public** (for public assets).

- **Database Configuration**: Rails uses a database for data storage, and you'll need to configure the database connection in the **config/database.yml** file. Rails supports multiple databases, including PostgreSQL, MySQL, and SQLite.

- **Migrations**: Rails provides a powerful feature called migrations to manage database schema changes over time. Migrations allow you to version-control and apply changes to your database schema using Ruby code.

- **Server**: You can run your Rails application locally during development using the built-in server. The command **rails server** or **rails s** starts the development server, allowing you to access your application in a web browser.

- **Development and Deployment**: Rails is well-suited for both development and deployment. You can develop your application locally and then deploy it to a web server using hosting services like Heroku, AWS, or a dedicated server.

Ruby on Rails streamlines web application development by providing a structured framework, sensible defaults, and a strong emphasis on best practices. It is widely used for building web applications, from small startups to large-scale enterprise projects, due to its productivity and the vibrant Ruby on Rails community.

10.3 Creating a Simple Web Application

1. **Generate a New Rails Application:**

   - Use the **rails new** command to create a new Rails application. Specify the name of your application as an argument.

   - This command sets up the directory structure, installs necessary gems, and creates initial configuration files.

2. **Define Routes:**

- In Rails, routes determine how HTTP requests are mapped to controller actions. You can define routes in the **config/routes.rb** file.

- Set up routes to map URLs to specific controller actions.

3. **Create Controllers:**

- Controllers are responsible for handling incoming HTTP requests, processing data, and rendering views. Create controllers using the **rails generate controller** command.

- Define actions within controllers to respond to different routes.

4. **Create Views:**

- Views are responsible for rendering HTML templates that

are sent back to the client's browser. Views are typically located in the **app/views** directory.

- Views can use embedded Ruby (ERB) or other templating languages to generate dynamic content.

5. **Define Models:**

- Models represent the data and business logic of your application. You can create models using the **rails generate model** command.

- Define associations between models, validations, and database tables in model files.

6. **Database Migrations:**

- Use Rails migrations (**rails generate migration**) to manage changes to the database schema.

- Run migrations (**rails db:migrate**) to apply schema changes to the database.

7. **Create Database Records:**

- Use the Rails console (**rails console**) to interact with the database and create records.

- Alternatively, create forms in your views to allow users to submit data that's stored in the database.

8. **Styling and Assets:**

- Customize the appearance of your application by adding CSS stylesheets to the **app/assets/stylesheets** directory.

- Include JavaScript files in the
  app/assets/javascripts
  directory if needed.

9. **Testing:**

   - Write unit tests and integration
     tests for your application using
     testing frameworks like RSpec
     or MiniTest.

   - Run tests (**rails test**) to ensure
     the application behaves as
     expected.

10. **Deployment:**

    - Choose a hosting provider for
      deploying your Rails
      application. Popular options
      include Heroku, AWS,
      DigitalOcean, and many more.

    - Configure the deployment
      environment, including setting
      up the production database.

- Deploy your application by pushing your code to a remote server.

11. **Monitoring and Maintenance:**

   - Implement monitoring and error tracking to identify and address issues in your application.

   - Regularly update gems and dependencies to keep your application secure and up to date.

12. **Scaling (if needed):**

   - If your application experiences increased traffic, consider scaling by adding more server resources or using load balancers.

Creating a simple web application in Ruby on Rails involves a series of steps, from setting up the project to deploying and maintaining it. Rails provides a framework that encourages best practices and accelerates the development process, making it a popular choice for web application development.

CHAPTER 11

Debugging and Testing

11.1 Debugging Techniques

- **Logging**: One of the simplest debugging techniques is adding log statements to your code. Use **puts** or a logging library like **Logger** to print variable values and messages at different points in your code to understand its flow.

- **Interactive Debugging**: Ruby has a built-in interactive debugger called **pry** (or **byebug** for Ruby 2.0+). You can insert breakpoints in your code and run it in debug mode to inspect variables and step through code execution.

- **Exception Handling**: Use **begin** and **rescue** blocks to catch exceptions and add debugging information to the rescue block. This can help identify the cause of errors and exceptions in your code.

- **Print Statements**: Inserting **puts** or **print** statements at various points in your code can help you track the execution flow and understand how values change during runtime.

- **Error Messages**: Pay attention to error messages and stack traces. They often provide valuable information about the location and nature of an error.

- **Rubber Duck Debugging**: Explain your code or problem to someone else (even an inanimate object like a rubber duck). The process of articulating the issue can often help you identify the problem.

- **Debugging Tools**: Ruby has debugging tools and IDEs that offer features like breakpoints, variable inspection, and real-time code execution analysis. Popular Ruby IDEs include RubyMine and Visual Studio Code with appropriate extensions.

11.2 Writing Basic Tests

- **Testing Frameworks**: Ruby has several testing frameworks, with RSpec and MiniTest being among the most popular. Choose a testing framework that fits your project's needs.

- **Unit Testing**: Write unit tests to verify that individual components of your code, such as methods or classes, behave correctly. Unit tests focus on testing isolated units of code in isolation from the rest of the application.

- **Integration Testing**: Integration tests check how different parts of your application work together. They ensure that the interactions between components function as expected.

- **Test Cases**: In your test suite, organize tests into test cases or contexts that group related tests together. This makes it easier to manage and run tests selectively.

- **Assertions**: Use assertions to specify the expected behavior of your code. Common assertions include checking for equality, inequality, truthiness, or specific exceptions.

- **Setup and Teardown**: Most testing frameworks allow you to define setup and teardown methods that run before and after each test case. Use these to prepare the environment and clean up resources.

- **Mocks and Stubs**: When testing code that interacts with external services or databases, use mocks and stubs to simulate their behavior, ensuring that tests remain isolated and repeatable.

- **Test Coverage**: Monitor test coverage to ensure that your tests are thorough and cover all critical parts of your code. Tools like SimpleCov can help you measure coverage.

- **Continuous Integration (CI)**: Set up a CI pipeline that automatically runs your tests whenever you push changes to your code repository. Popular CI services for Ruby projects include Travis CI, CircleCI, and GitHub Actions.

- **Test-Driven Development (TDD)**: Consider adopting TDD, a development approach where you write tests before implementing the corresponding code. TDD can lead to more reliable and maintainable code.

Debugging and testing are essential practices in software development that help identify and prevent bugs and ensure the reliability of your code. By mastering debugging techniques and writing effective tests, you can build robust and maintainable Ruby applications.